LINES

LINES
NO FIRE COULD BURN

John Hejduk

THE MONACELLI PRESS

First published in the United States of America in 1999 by
The Monacelli Press, Inc.
10 East 92nd Street, New York, New York 10128.

Library of Congress Cataloging-in-Publication Data
Hejduk, John, date.
Lines : no fire could burn / by John Hejduk.
p. cm.
ISBN 1-58093-038-7
I. Title.
PS3558.E472L56   1999
811'.54—dc21   99-29211

Printed and bound in the United States

Designed by Kim Shkapich

Dedicated to David Shapiro

CHRIST IN PRAGUE
 —David Shapiro   *13*

 1   TO ABSORB THE SINS OF MAN   *14*

 2   WILL THERE BE BLOOD   *15*

 3   DIG INTO THE EARTH   *16*

 4   ODOR OF HIS HAVOC   *17*

 5   THE WEIGHTS OF HEARTS   *18*

 6   NOT YET A WARNING   *20*

 7   HELLS ANGEL BURNS   *21*

 8   MAGNIFICENT NIGHT ANGEL   *22*

 9   ALL THIS BEFORE ME   *23*

 10 THE RETURNING ANGEL   *24*

 11 I BRING TO OTHERS   *25*

 12 FILLED WITH FLAME   *27*

 13 A SHADOW FELL   *28*

 14 FIRST LINE OF DAWN   *29*

 15 A METAL FLOWER   *30*

 16 NIGHT GARDEN   *31*

 17 THE LAST SUPPER   *32*

 18 THE UNEARTHLY WEIGHT   *34*

 19 A LANDSCAPE   *35*

20	CUT IN THE SOIL	36
21	WITHIN	38
22	INSIDE OF ME	39
23	THE DEPOSITION	40
24	PERMANENT REMEMBRANCE	42
25	THE BODY AND WOUNDS	44
26	HIS ELONGATED BODY	45
27	THE DARKNESS	47
28	HER DEATH	48
29	THE UNDERTOW OF THOUGHT	49
30	SOUNDS OF CREATION	53
31	IN ITS SILENCE	55
32	OCEAN LIQUIDS	56
33	WHO WILL BELIEVE IN ME	57
34	PASSAGE	59
35	IN HIS FATHERS HOUSE	60
36	RAIN OF PETALS	61
37	THE GREEN ROOM	63
38	THE PANTHERS SILENCE	65

39	A BLUE ROSE	67
40	THE LAKE	69
41	THE WALLPAPER	71
42	GLACIERS IN THE SUN	72
43	NO FIRE COULD BURN	74
44	THEN AN EXPLOSION	75
45	IN UNMOVING BLOOD STILLED	76
46	I WILL BUILD IT OF STONE	78
47	HOLDING THEM CLOSE	80
48	TO FRESH COLD	82
49	IN NATURES FIELDS	83
50	HIS SHADOW CUTS	85
51	WAS THERE TIME	86
52	THIS DAY TO MOURN	87
53	LEAVING THE EYES OPEN	88
54	INTERIOR STONES IN THE NIGHT	90
55	RESPLENDENT GLORY	92
56	YOUR CONTEMPLATIVE SADNESS	93
57	AND TO SOLITUDE	95

58   CASKETED BONES   96

59   LET US RETURN   98

60   SOUND OF THE SEA   100

61   A CHURCH SPIRE ROSE   102

62   THE SWEET JUICE BLED   103

63   OF SHADES AND SHADOWS   105

64   IT HARDLY FLOWED   107

65   YOUR ANGUISH BURNING   108

66   IN TIME OVER LONG TIME   110

67   HIS SOUL WAS DANCING   112

68   AND WHAT ARE THEY   114

69   THE CLIFFS OF LE HARVE   116

70   IN THE SPRING   118

71   THE AIR BECAME COLD   119

72   PURE BLUE WAS SAVED   120

73   DEATH OF THE VIRGIN   121

     THE FUNERAL OF JAN PALACH
                —David Shapiro   123

     ILLUSTRATIONS   127

for Gloria Hejduk

CHRIST IN PRAGUE

Christ collects his own blood
In a rudimentary chalice
Outlined by a childish master
His skin is grey like patched-up plaster
The angels who surround us are young
Their wings are fish
And buckles around their neck
With keyholes to the gate
Brown blood keeps falling from his nailed head
Panicked and sad, another victim
Black blood keeps falling from one hand like paint
And red blood from his beard
Like crayon blotches
The blood is the color after all of his
    excellent long hair
It falls like tears from the crown of thorns
When the blood reaches the cup it turns golden
And the gold sun behind him shines with triple flowers

—David Shapiro

TO ABSORB THE SINS OF MAN

To absorb the sins of man
into a body while it loses its blood
a sacrifice of the beyond the human
his mother never to see Hell
yet to see him crucified
from original bliss to lament
he from resurrection to ascension — *himmelfart*
blue veil for her golden disc for him
she broken hearted twice
he once alive on the cross
he once dead on the cross
know the pain of womans heart

WILL THERE BE BLOOD

She sensed that she would be told
she looked out into the garden
it was not the same
its color had changed
into a golden sepia
and the enclosing cypress trees
had turned black
she felt an unease
the calm air became agitated
the landscape transformed
into a blue gray without sounding
an immense splendid glorious angel
appeared before her
I bring you an announcement
that will change everything
it is about a birth
she lowered her veil
and asked the angel
and who will bring
the announcement of a death
anyone who is capable of love
will there be blood in both cases

DIG INTO THE EARTH

Angel you are beautiful
I did not think you would be so tall
and your eyes so dark
you look tired. . . . From such a long journey
the feathers of your wings
are made up of more than one color
they are almost twelve inches long
your hair is like frozen silk
how strange. . . . Your skin is the color
of white marble
your robe fabricated of the finest strands
your hands are elegant and long
you bring me a message

Then something terrible happened
the wings of the angel began to flutter
at great speed and irregular beat
creating distortion in their shape
then the unearthly sound came
from the mouth of the angel
a screeching lament
its eyes receding into a darkness
it fell to its knees
and began to dig into the Earth

4

ODOR OF HIS HAVOC

Do you think I always fly smoothly
in the winds of God
that I can always be in touch with Earth
think you not that I not shiver
in altitudes cold ice forms in my hair
my eyebrows are covered with snow
my tears do drop in temperature
do you know the faith it takes
to move my heavy wings
are you aware my eyes cry in their darkness
when black clouds interrupt my stability
Gods commands must be answered instantaneously
when the Angel of Death makes his move
do you know the odor of his havoc
his reaping immense his precision unrelenting
there is no evasion we must fly alongside
the cries of the damned
have you ever seen the Angel of Hell
fly along the red flames of damnation
you to be saved and you not
what lists are prepared that the Styx boatman
makes no mistake the feathers of our wings
cover the alphabet. . . . Yet some slip through
we common angels are thought to be three-quarter size
yet we carry Gods words weight
with one angry outburst he is capable of
imploding our imagined universe
our wings are heavy with the souls of the dead

THE WEIGHTS OF HEARTS

What causes all this sound
and the cacophonic disarray
within the clouds suddenly
filled with angels and light
are they lost or have they lost
their angelic sense of mute
celebrations . . . the airs jubilations
foretells of a coming
judgements structure is being built
the waves are touching
the undersides of the night clouds
Gabriels memory is being ignited
he vaguely remembers his original flight
to the Virgin and her questions about blood
her early forsaken blood transferred
to a Cross on lonely Calvary

why do these angels dance in the sky
have they forgotten his and his Mothers pain
is it not better to silently float in the sky
in reverence to a soul that encompassed our sins
do you not hear the mounting thunderous sound
of those attempting to leave Hell
crying for forgiveness their souls to be levitated
erase the baroque ceilings
so their pleas can reach to the possible
space of forgiveness
volcanic rock eventually reaches the sea
where it warms the ocean of cold doubt
angels be done with lightweightness
and take on the weights of hearts

NOT YET A WARNING

The falling snow became a veil
for winter Jerusalem
the Judean landscape
a white undulating ocean
the vertical black tree trunks
not yet a warning
then. . . .
Christ and his disciples
moved down a hill
between the vertical dark lines
through the cold dry air
Jesus was shouting into the heavens
in a language strange
no one could understand
I will be betrayed
there will be
an enormous shift within the Earth
and all the angels
will come unto me

HELLS ANGEL BURNS

The darkest blue night
of the blackest crucifixion
where the blood remains red
as the tears of his Mothers lament
thicken into an indescribable blue
Hells red dies down to burnt embers
and Hells angel burns
the blue filter dissolves
exposing a black and white world
where a God has been crucified

MAGNIFICENT NIGHT ANGEL

After death where does the soul go
does it remain in the last resting place
of the silent body
if it leaves when does it leave
is there resistance to departure
does it leave by itself
is there a guide

It rises and moves upwards
to soul heights
it remains as long as it has to
there is no resistance to departure
it leaves with an angel
the magnificent night angel
who gathers throughout the night
till the light of all dawns
it sends out wave lines of force
announcing its coming
when it arrives the air
simply becomes heavier
and the angel more thoughtful

ALL THIS BEFORE ME

I remember such strange things
my memory is the deepest on Earth
I remember the taste of your milk
purest of liquids
I remember the softness of your breast
its moving gentleness
and the hands
that placed it in my seeking mouth
joy and calmness
I remember as a boy seeing you take your shawl
from your head releasing the flow of your hair
you even smiled at my astonishment
you brought me close and allowed me to touch it
I remember the kiss you gave me
when I told you I wanted to be a carpenter
am I seeing all this before me
for the first time
the miracle I remember most was your voice
it can only be described as melodious
its sound carried into the chambers of ones heart
forever resonant . . . glorious

THE RETURNING ANGEL

Angel come near
we met some time ago
your message made me
think of other things
angel come near
so I can now embrace you
and I can now touch your feathers
is it possible that you can give me one
I will put it in my small casket
angel come near
so I can look into your heavenly eyes
they are dark receding conical shapes
disappearing into your vanishing perspectives
to a point of silver
angel come near
so I can run my fingers through
your soft flaxen hair
let me hold your hands in my hands
they are cold let me give them some warmth
angel come near
so I can see the curvatures of your lips
they are the color of opals
your breath is the odor of recent cut wheat
mixed with roses
angel come near
so I can give you a gentle
parting kiss
before you return home

I BRING TO OTHERS

The fallen angel brought many things
down . . . with him
he wrenched night from day
and made it darker
he gathered night so rapidly
that the stars were caught in his domain
they were the angels that inhabited
the edge of Heaven
the flickering light they gave off
were their cries for help
during the day they could not be seen
the moon was his night light
when he searched for lost souls
when he found one
his black wings completely enfolded
the lost one
then he held the victim in his arms
and flew to the edge of the flames of Hell
he could never find a lost angel
he knew the outer angels were there
for when it rained it was their tears
that fell on his black feathers

11

when it snowed they were shedding their sorrows
which the dark angel melted in his fire
sometimes during the day he hid in the
black clouds of a storm with the faint hope
that he would be readmitted
he was an angel shark always in motion flying
when in pain because of his fate
he shouted to the Heavens
   ... God help me ... release me from the suffering
I bring to others

FILLED WITH FLAME

You fell into unmeasurable depths
you stole night from day
you moved so rapidly that some angels are lost
at the edge of Hell
I hear their cries and lament
during the night you search for them
with a demonic thirst
the fires of Hell almost touch the tips
of your extended wings in your foul flights
you hide in black storm clouds
you cannot be seen but your odor
is in the air
you ask to return yet you do not believe
we believe you spread evil and chaos
and your heart is filled with flame
you would set afire all the clouds in Heaven
you captured the moon to give you night light
you are jealous of the sun
you are the brother of the shark
you are to blame

13

A SHADOW FELL

A shadow fell over the angel of darkness
above him flew a golden feathered angel
in a blue robe with woven white stars
the Angel of Death ascended so swiftly
from below that the angel above was unaware
until it was too late
the black winged angel caught him
and spun him around on his back
they were joined in four winged flight
the golden wing was quickly broken
the stricken angel fell down into the sea
and was washed on to the shore
where its life left it
it died in the shallow water of the shore
not far away the bronze statute of Poseidon
was in the sand staring at the angel
through its empty eye sockets
a womans voice could be heard in the distance

FIRST LINE OF DAWN

Angel I have searched the beach everywhere
and I have found you lying here in the sand
they said you had drowned and it is true
the particles of the wet sand are silver
they reflect the moonlight your feathers
are a luminescent blue a golden crab
clings to you as the tide gently covers its
shell I separate the phosphorescent seaweed
from your hair there too are red starfish
your eyes stare up at me in their complexity
as I close them with the palm of my hand
a white cloud in the night covers the moonlight
it is impossible to lament an annunciating angel
for its abundant joy overcomes death
the tide is rising and soon will take you out to sea
I will wait with you at the edge of the water
until the time comes for you to depart from me
and now I will kiss your alabaster lips
as the first line of dawn ascends
I fold my hands over yours reluctant to let go

A METAL FLOWER

The indigo night faded
into a pewter dawn
he looked over the placid sea
it moved slightly at times
the mountains were barren
and dark ochre
his lips murmured to the waiting water
the sea turned into a volume of mercury
he raised his eyes upward
to a sky of thickening clouds
they were composed of flowers
a multitude of subdued colors
rapidly passing overhead
they fell like a heavy rain
onto the silver sea
as the flowers touch the surface
they transformed into metal
and reflected the miracle
of colored pigment
a sea of solidifying liquid
the sun rose and put a final glaze
on the flowered surface
he walked out onto the sea
and picked up a metal rose
which then changed in his hand
to its original state
and gave off the scent of forgiveness
the enclosed seas solidity liquefied
as the wind moved his boat
to the blossoming shore

NIGHT GARDEN

I walk in this night garden
and know I will be betrayed
his embrace lingers on my cloth
his whispers have already begun
to close my ears yet I can still
hear the song of the nightingale
can you hear it so far away
in this dark I can hardly make
out the moving shades yet I see
the black cypress imperceptibly
swaying as the cold passes
the coins they gave him
are like pieces of ice
and when the deed is done
they will turn to fire and
scorch the Earth no flowers
will grow there only abandonment
look I have found a red rose
in this garden of sorrows
its aroma announces my death
to the East the sun rises and
the moon gives one last kiss
to the soon to be silent
night garden give me your shroud
when you see it again
you will remember me

THE LAST SUPPER

The Disciples lifted the white cloth
and floated it over the table
the material was held taut
then lowered
compressing the air
between cloth and wood
bread and pewter plates
were put in place
flasks of liquid
reflected the light
wine spilled
on the white fabric
staining the surface
the twelve men sat down
and waited
they looked at each other
when Christ entered
they rose
the last sun faded
behind the head of Jesus
the light failed
as night penetrated
shadows softened the air

as the last supper commenced
the angels in the sky
disappeared
creating a vacuum
snow fell
on the olive trees
an echo covered the Earth
a restlessness descended
within his sleeping Mother
her heart filled with blood
tears flowed
beneath her closed eyes
and filled her internal cavities
as she awoke
her voice sounded
my Son where are you
the blackness of the red roses
in the dark green room
illuminated her soul
of sorrow
a lone angel moved its wings
to begin flight

THE UNEARTHLY WEIGHT

The Cross was too heavy
and he fell
blood moved from his
bent knees
on to the rough stone
his Mother sprung
from the onlooking crowd
to his side
lifted his head
and looked
deep into his
blood soaked eyes
I am your Mother
and I am with you
my beloved Son
he lifted one arm
balanced the wood Cross
on his indented shoulder
and continued towards
the site of his death
his Mother grasped
the Cross
splinters entered her
pleading hands
she fell
and was quickly lifted up
by souls of the street
her heart obtained
an unearthly weight
the weight of the Cross

A LANDSCAPE

He felt the Cross rising
and the blood escaping
through his hands and feet
the nails gave him earthly pain
his horizontality becoming upright
a horseman speared his side
his skin was stained
the entering metal
reflecting a diminishing light
he opened his eyes
and was able to see
the landscape of sorrow
his Mother had collapsed
and he sensed his own implosion
he heard last word sounds
and was unable to distinguish
if they were his own Mothers
or the ultimate
of the soul leaving

20

CUT IN THE SOIL

The soldier removed his spear
from Christs side
after having committed its opening
he pulled hard on his horses reins
and moved the animal backwards
making a path through the assembly
of mourners
the horse slipped and fell
with its rider
the spear released from his metal hand
its point entered the Earth
and the blood it contained
was absorbed beneath the ground
to his astonishment
the blade turned pure white
in the vanishing light
he uprighted his horse
remounted

and rode slowly away
dragging the spear at his side
the point slashed the Earth
as it made a line
from the cut in the soil
there gushed up
vertical fountains of blood
the horse and rider
became covered in its substance
they were one mass volume of dark red
the soldier jolted the horse into a gallop
charging into a wind
what was seen by those who witnessed it
was an amorphous shape
streaking along side an elevation of night blue
and the inability of the observers
to distinguish the unearthly howling
of man beast and wind

WITHIN

As earthness faded
he heard the thunder
of his heart
a heavy thick sound
his ears then closed
to all external
he felt his blood move
in extraordinary flow
he sensed his ultimate
within
his heart and blood
stopped
he died
his vision inverted
for the first time
he felt the weight
of his soul

INSIDE OF ME

My son on the Cross
can you hear me
I am witness to your agony
I am here with you
my son on the Cross
my pain knows your pain
it has happened
yet I am unable to believe
my son on the Cross
I love you so much
you have received wounds
unimaginable blood everywhere
your beloved are here with you
the birds have flown away in horror
my son on the Cross
please speak to me
so I can have your voice
inside of me for eternity

THE DEPOSITION

They reached Christs outstretched arms
at the same moment
and gasped at the
horizontal perspective
the nails penetrated
his ash palms
perpendicular to the wood
the sight gave pain
to their already constricted
hearts
their souls became
incomprehensible
the ropes around
their wet shoulders
slid off the skin
burning the surface
they looked up
at the Crown of Thorns
and saw the blood tips
his hair flowed
over his silent ears
his eyes stared down
at the stained Earth below
through the dust
covered liquid
his beard becoming marble

brushed his dry lips
his mouth open
they believed they heard
a last word
the white gray clouds
wiped the moon clean
and left it black
the beads of sweat
on their foreheads
turned to ice
chilling what remained
of their sorrowful souls
they removed the nails
and new blood flowed
the wounds opened up
as rose petals do
they lowered
him slowly
from the Cross
into his Mothers arms
her lament could be heard
across the barren valley
the sun rose rapidly
driving out the moon

PERMANENT REMEMBRANCE

They carried him
down the hill
the Cross was left
in the dawns awakening
the three punctures
in the wood
were surrounded by
dry blood
the sun did not rise
on that drastic day
the moon abandoned
the stained Earth
there were no possibilities
of shadows
and no need of shade
wind ceased
and the air became thick

his weight increased
as the bearers descended
his Mothers face
contained sorrows
that existed since antiquity
her heart an ocean of pain
filling her internal being
she released an inner sigh
a sound that froze
to a stillness
the angels in flight
made God tremble
from the immensity
of the agony
permanent remembrance
was created then

25

THE BODY AND WOUNDS

He felt her
gently remove the Crown of Thorns
and heard the sounds of her sorrow
her arms comforted
his former agony
she held him close
as they washed
his body and wounds
and he sensed
the soft cloth
they covered him with
he knew
they were lifting him
and placing him within granite
which would evaporate
when he rose
to the startled heavens

HIS ELONGATED BODY

They lifted her son
and gently placed him
in the granite tomb
it was cold to their touch
as they moved the lid
over him
enclosing
his elongated body
as soon as the internal
darkness was complete
his wounds began to close
his Mother and those
who loved him
walked into the night
her blue cloak covering her
became luminous
grieving arms
were put around her
she looked up
into the stars
it is then that he
began to stir within
he heard her
weeping
into the far distant
Earth

he felt tears
move up into his eyes
he opened his vision
and saw within the darkness
that he was surrounded
by red roses thornless
their aroma entered his nostrils
which breathed again
then all the flowers of Earth
gave him their fragrance
he inhaled the gift of their
abundance
within his mouth he sensed
the aftertaste of blood
which immediately
filled his lips with
the sweetness of a new wine
he raised his hands up
to the low surface above him
it was eternally light
he knew he was free and blessed
Heaven and Earth
awaited him

THE DARKNESS

His eyes opened
he was sealed
he heard the dripping
of cave water
he felt the cavities
of the dried wounds
with a melodious voice
he called to the Heavens
to release him from
this darkness
suddenly the boulder
enclosing the entry
burst out with such fury
he could feel the immense
suction surrounding his body
he gave no resistance
to his upwardboundness

HER DEATH

Her death came
when he called
the clouds remained still . . .
as his voice
sounded down to Earth
reaching
her beloved gentleness
she smiled at
the sublime joining

The sun retracted its flame
the moon received all shadows
the sea froze at the shore
and the rose bloomed

THE UNDERTOW OF THOUGHT

The moon accompanies
Christs awakening agony
the suns rays cut their own volume
into a folded steel plate
which captures the particles
of the moons afterglow
revealing the Crown of Thorns
as points of reflected blood
congealing into an opaque
chalk substance
which denies flood and fire
he forgives others pain
his own frozen
his Mother draws within herself
all the shades of Earths blue
lamenting the loss
the sea hides the fallen sun
leaving iridescent crystals
anticipating the feathers
of future angel wings
the metallic sun blades
puncture the moist Earth
providing seed sepulchers

The day the sea
became mercury
was the thickest
day of time
hours fell into depths
as pellets of memory
ship bows dipped
awashed
in sliding silver
seeking
a multitude of balances
only to drown again
with their crew
the Captain murmured
all is well
the Albatross turned dark plum
and bled indigo
the dead pulled
the buoys below
as undersea bells
red and black
submerged

The eclipse covered
the suns surface
darkening the sphere
intensifying
the circumferences
edge light
the moon became black
as did Christs face
the inner spirit
burst forward
as a flowering of forgiveness
and the storms tide receded
leaving water pools of hope
and streams of thought
the sound of the undertow
could faintly be heard
in the distant seascape
and fishermen
wailed into mornings night

Christs passage through Hell
moved Earths plates
to extremities
time shifted
perspective vanished into pain

The first to reach Christ
on the Cross
after climbing the ladder
shouted
into the ear
of the crucified one
"Jesus.... Can you hear me?"

SOUNDS OF CREATION

The metal spikes
were driven through
his hands and his feet
a spear into his side
into his very soul
with those ferocious acts
pain was absorbed
into an immense silence
and the counter force
of meaning. . . . Of love and
forgiveness
was changed for eternity
churches would be built
over centuries
sculptures would be made
placed on and in cathedrals
landscapes would be awakened
by their presence
rose windows would flood
interior darkness with the
sacred light of color
painters would paint
the images of Christs time
and of his Mothers gentleness
books would be written

with miraculous letters and words
songs would be sung
in his glory
and music would be composed
to fill our hearts with the
sounds of creation

IN ITS SILENCE

Christ spoke softly
to God in Heaven
asking him to stop
the bleeding
where is the bleeding
I see it not
answered the Heavenly
Father
it is inside
replied Jesus
internally flooding me
a wind passed over
his organs
drying his enclosure
his eyes then witnessed
the sun being hidden by
the flight of agitated angels
later he could only remember
the intensity of the colors
dark apricot and plum red
he sensed his pain
was moving towards the past
and that he could
give comfort
to the cries
coming from the Earth
Heaven would wait
in its silence

OCEAN LIQUIDS

The sun and the moon
touched at a tangent point
on the horizon line
of the still sea
and exchanged their weights
during the blackness of night
white clouds moved
forward
from the deep perspective
of a planar sky
a pewter fin broke the
flatness of the water
and all the stars
gathered together
forming a sphere
of light
while blood rose
from the phosphorescent depths
through the silent
ocean liquids

WHO WILL BELIEVE IN ME

What has happened
everything
where am I
everywhere
when do I speak
whenever
how is it
that I see day and night
simultaneously
that is your vision
the sun and moon are gone
yes
what replaces them
your own circles and spheres
they are too immense
to recreate
then paint them in the sky
one red or orange
one yellow or white
what will happen
they will materialize
and the stars
they are former angels
am I in Heaven
you have been
always on Earth
who will believe in me
almost all

what will they do
they will pray to you
in what way
in all ways
what will I give them
yourself
what happened
you were crucified
there was great pain
unimaginable pain

PASSAGE

The cellist moved his sound
into the soul of Christ
evoking the agony
and the forgiving
simultaneously
Jesus looked at him
through eyes
of vanishing centuries
and long ago memories
where the blackness
of tree trunks
were darker than
printers ink
and the sheets of music
contained embalmed sound
Jesus followed the score
and hummed in
all silences
so that the composer
could reflect space
filled with the aroma
of black roses
and sepia women
our Lord opened up
the gardens for
the female voice
accompanied by the cellist
and his haunting bow
gliding over the strings
of a mauve Heaven
where music had risen

IN HIS FATHERS HOUSE

The sun burst through
the black sky
a white blazing meteorite
with a long tail of stars
moved in at a fierce speed
then disappeared into
the flames of the
expanding ball of fire
impregnation was complete
the receding moon
through immense suction
pulled all the remaining stars
into its vortex
they vanished through
a spiralling funnel of air
the oceans of the Earth
fell into a vacated universe
leaving dry cavities of sea beds
and all the uprooted trees
flew within the cacophony
of the disoriented winds
man could not be found
and only the cries of a woman
could be heard
all this was dreamed by Jesus
before he awoke in his Fathers house

RAIN OF PETALS

He lay down
in the softness
of the grass
stretched his arms out
perpendicular to his body
and looked directly up
to a sky turned blood red
by a rejected sun which
set the cypresses
afire
the wind interweaved
the dark green branches
with the flames
the black tree trunks
turned white before
transforming to ash
which covered him
his eyes were
blue crystals in a
smoldering mound
the red of the Heavens
started to crack
and formed into a
multitude of roses
which began to fall
to the Earth
as a rain of
moist velvet petals

ash and roses now
covered
his horizontal form
he sat upright
petal and ash
enmeshed in his hair
he then raised himself
straight up
and spoke into the
flowering air
I Am Jesus

THE GREEN ROOM

There are moments
that only time remembered
as when he brought
the rose to his lips
and the scent entered
his mouth
the red powder mixed
with his hearts blood
to enlarge the gray
veins near the surface
of his skin
his smile made
his cheek bones rise
and his almond shaped
eyelids slightly close
intensifying the silver
spheres of his pupils
floating in a pure white
porcelain liquid
his hands and fingers
were extremely long
he could imagine the hands
of the future Braque
his brushes beside him
they were centuries apart
Braque talked about
his paintings
Jesus listened

37

for he then knew
what was to happen
before he left
he arranged a bowl of fruit
into a still life
and painted a wood pear gold
a large purple bird
flew into the dark green room
then became enmeshed
in the arabesque wallpaper
Braque fell asleep in his chair
within his silence
he witnessed
the crucifixion of Christ

THE PANTHERS SILENCE

When crossing the lemon grove
the shadows of the leaves
were lit by the pearl moon
turning the nights Earth
into a palette of moving undulations
the cypress trees remained
black in their geometric stillness
the Disciples pulled their cloaks
tight around their chillness
fires were started
on the distant plateaus
the Dead Sea appeared
as a plane of mercury
it was then that Jesus hummed
a tone filled with sadness
reaching back
to the birth of time
the men were startled
by the soulful inner lament
when they passed the cypress trees
they closed their eyes
for the branches were bleeding
the disciples looked back
the lemons had transformed
into roses of pure blue
by then Christs voice was singing
a song of the miraculous love of women
the sound was mysterious joyful and lovingly

sensible as it passed over
the melancholy landscape
they had never heard him sing before or after
although he continued
to remember the words he sung
he was unable to write them down

He focused on the snow
falling on the Judean hills
his hearing concentrated
on the lions roar
and the panthers silence
he marvelled at the Earths abundance
and the music in its heart
Bach wrote the first notes of the mass

A BLUE ROSE

They extracted the wood Cross
from the damp Earth
still blood mixed in the soil
they lifted it upon their shoulders
and carried it to the sea
where they put it on a boat
which later during its voyage
slid the Cross into the waters
as the ship passed Malta
the Cross floated for many days
in the blue waves
at one time a current brought it
to the lower depths where
it passed the bronze statute
of Poseidon lying in the sand
eventually the Cross came to rest
on the shore outside of Ostia
it was covered with seaweed
when the fishermen found it
others transported it to Florence
and hid it in a place which centuries later
was to become the Medici Chapel
where Michelangelo created
his mysterious tombs
the Last Judgement was fermenting
in his soul
the Cross was never found

there stands a tall Cross
on a remote sand dune near Ostia Antica
totally covered in black and red roses
a woman wearing an indigo cloak
stands by watching the flowers fade
she remembers the first time she saw a blue rose
it was at dusk in Egypt
a snake surrounded it

THE LAKE

They were walking through a woods
filled with black tree trunks
thick leaves of dark green overhead
permitted a plum vermilion light
to penetrate at various intervals
to turn the ground into a golden red
when he halted them back
to a stillness
their white robes hung as vertical shrouds
a pewter disc slowly spun behind his head
which had a wreath of purple and blue
flowers around its circumference
the auburn black beard
made his face skin seem
a chalk white his lips pink grey
his eyes cobalt blue
reflecting diamond points of light
which went back into his internal space
for thousands of years in distance
some yards down the slope
to the lake a doe
slowly approached the clear water
a cloth of dark mauve
with small white Crosses imprinted on it
was over her back and sides
the deer bent its neck to drink
after drinking it turned to face
the men hiding in the snow

in the almost invisible
woods of greyness
before their eyes the doe
transformed into a young woman
of a haunting demeanor
I am your daughter she said
to the vanishing figure in the woods
in faint voice he replied
I am your father
her robe fell
as she moved backwards
into the lakes waters
she sung the song
of all dawns

THE WALLPAPER

Jesus saw that the large brown bird
was entangled in the pattern of
the wallpaper painted by Braque
and he was saddened by its plight
the painter was looking forlornly
at the wall
he spoke to the figure who had
entered and appeared in his room
you have come to see my paintings
I have come to release the bird
from your pigments
Lord let me mix you a color that
those on Earth have never seen
Braque did so
when Jesus looked at the miraculous color
he said to the old painter it is seen
in Heaven and now it is on Earth
Braque fell asleep in his chair
his long fingers held the brushes
he used to paint the color for Jesus
in the dawn when he awoke
the painted wallpaper
no longer held the bird in flight
in its place was a disc of the color
made in Heaven and Earth

GLACIERS IN THE SUN

Jesus I have seen all there is to see
of all the works devoted to your love
and what did you see
miraculous things
did you see the beech tree in the fall
in the snow
I have seen rivers of ice flowing
out to sea
did you see the Dead Sea and the Judean Hills
I have seen what man had made
to remember you
I have heard women's voices
singing great song works composed about
your time on Earth
the longest time imaginable
how long have you traveled the Earth
as long as you have been in Heaven
did you see the beech tree covered in ice
I have seen the mountains melt

did you see the wheat fields in the wind
I have seen the desert in the moonlight
did you see the beech tree in the spring
I have seen the jungles in the rain
and the glaciers in the sun
and the marshes in the fog
did you see the beech tree in August
I have seen the beech tree struck by lightning
what is it that you have seen
that has the most substance
it is that which I can never see
but has the most substance
and what is the name of that substance
My Lord it is called the soul
I felt it as I lay under the oldest beech tree
as evening eased into night

NO FIRE COULD BURN

If judgement in time postponed
and God had wished command
the moons cold may have engulfed
he of the Cross no fire could burn
the fiery sun blazed the wood to ash
releasing Christs earthly stay
rising swiftly upward cloud protected
ejecting agonies memory
as all wounds wind healed
blood turned into rain wine
washing the land to accept forgiveness
the night did fade into mornings glory
if judgement in time postponed

THEN AN EXPLOSION

The Heavenly Father sounded
a forthcoming command tumultuous
that thunder became enlightenment
he crushed lightning bolts in hand
distributing golden shards of invitation
to winged creatures of holiness
come on to me in evenings decent was his word
when the new sun flew upward
all mature angels blocked out shadow
and shade leaving moon disc illuminations
wing headed angel children frightening
Earths man and beast
wood ships move out to sea in midnight black
the lions dug holes in terra cotta firmness
a distant roar came out from the horizon
he shed his death in a resurrection
that announced eternities presence
from a womans voice a song
that reached an intensity in pitch
of the harmonic fluctuations of angel wings
during Heavens accelerations
her continued song sound
haunting calm soft silence

Then an explosion
that emptied space
of stars and light
and left only
the pure possibility of love

45

IN UNMOVING BLOOD STILLED

I have seen you crucified
a thousand times
above altars
I have seen the light
of rose windows
moving over your body
and I have seen priests
drink wine from a chalice
and giving the host
to open mouths
I have seen you made of stone
and metal and of wood
I have seen your face
change many times
over centuries
it has made tears fall
I have seen your crucified body
in unmoving blood stilled
I believe in the many colors
of the blood
that the painters have mixed
I have looked into your eyes
that have confronted me
in their opacity
I have witnessed the flush
in your cheek bones
painted by an artist who loved you
he sung a song to the gift of pigment

I quietly observed
the gentleness in which he applied
the satin finish upon your forehead
I was astonished
by the many contours and flows
of your carved out hair of wood
your ashen face reminded me
of dusks descent and mornings prayer
I saw you once made entirely of steel
I always looked up
to your transforming size
I awaited a sound
from your hardly opened lips
and I looked for your hidden heart
your volumes flooded me
with your sacred forgiveness
my soul could imagine unseen works
I stood alone
in your cathedrals
of evening vespers
where candles
flickered in thick glass
and total darkness
eventually came
I awoke at the first note
of the thunderous organs sound
announcing soul judgements

I WILL BUILD IT OF STONE

He spoke in an almost audible voice
a voice of vespers
I met one who experienced shipwreck
his captain made a vow
when he witnessed the birth
of a Hell
a volcano pushed through
the surface of a disoriented sea
building a fire that challenged the sun
their ship disintegrated
imploding as it descended
a great suction made the sand cloud
and forever hid the ship
the waves wrote words of salvation
the captain spoke in a calm voice
I will build a stone cathedral
off the coast of Africa
I will build in honor of the Virgin
I will make a miracle of construction
I will build it of stone
and it will be undersea

a great enclosing jetty will surround it
the blue Mediterranean
will fill its liquid volume
a womb of watery space
will accept the penetrating light of the sun
magnificent cables will ring
the massive bell
thick sound will rise
and break the seas surface
sending birds into sinking clouds
when will you start
it is already finished
have you not seen it
as I spoke to you
did you not sense its glory
and were you not overwhelmed
into silence with the vision
of the enclosed waters
and the holy Mother
and the creation of
the Son of God

HOLDING THEM CLOSE

In the mountains
near the glacier
a lost angel flew
into a small church
during vespers
it was agitated
and frightened
it gave off sad shrieks
its wings flapped
in disorder
some golden feathers
falling to the stone floor
the angels black eyes
revealed its terror
the priest tried
to calm it through
words of kindness
its shadow moved
rapidly on the
white washed walls
its wings touched
the stations of the Cross
the angel swiftly rose
to the roofs rafters
alighted and looked

with phosphorescent eyes
at the commotion below
the parishioners started
to frantically ring
the church bell
and the thunder sound
jolted the winged figure
it flew down
to the life sized crucifixion
suspended above the altar
the lost angel wrapped
its arms and wings
around the suffering Christ
and with all its strength
released Christ and the Cross
from its supports
holding them close
it flew out of the church
into the night
upwards towards the white moon
throughout the thickening dawn
the church organ could be heard
across the valley
its sound was
a terrifying lament

48

TO FRESH COLD

He went down
to Hell
and knew them not
forgiveness expanded
mercy beg them different
no soul permitted
that suffering
he chilled fires
to embers disappearance
through eyes indifferent
to punishments argument
he rushed in roses
cleansing the hurt
restoring possibilities blush
he raised the sea
to fresh cold
he banished impossible dusk
for sight to be restored
he listened for cloud opening
he led them to
the voice of yes
Heaven help them

The sweetness of days dawning

IN NATURES FIELDS

Are your eyes yours
when you see over centuries
of time so many
images of your face of pain
do you desire to see the one
that has painted your dying
do you desire to speak to the
sculptors that depicted your agony
how many bloods painted
were not the color of your blood
how many wood Crosses
were constructed in a thousand years
that did not come from your
beloved landscape O Judea
did you see yourself
where did your youth go
did you recognize your Mother
in the so many statues of the Virgin
was her hair the texture of your hair
when you looked at your duplicated eyes
did your own bring up tears
were you able to feel the cold of morning
in paintings of Judean skies
how many mornings have risen
in the dark paintings of Calvary
were you astonished

49

by the number of cathedrals that
were built in deep reverence
for your sacrifice and love
my God the onrush of cathedrals
land lighthouses for lost souls
and other things too holy spirit
onrush of cathedrals
mans glacial stone
to be placed in natures fields
flying buttresses
blessed by angels
descending in nights blue
ascending in dawns gray
do you remember that northern blue
do you remember the blue of your Mothers cloth
can you find it in years of paintings
do you want to
when you look at the deposition
through funneling centuries
do you feel your own weight
being lifted so your Mother
can cradle you again
do you remember your Mother
looking that way

I remember all

HIS SHADOW CUTS

Judea
a Son has risen
he walks the snow covered
hill plateaus
to find the sea of Galilee
have you witnessed
his face of tears
Judea
as he walks
his arms are opened
for an embrace
his shadow cuts
through the Earth
Judea
his hair blows
in the wind
he opens his lips
to sing a song
his eyes glow
at its melodic sound
Judea
his pace quickens
in the melting snow
his heart has
run out of time
Judea
a Son has risen

WAS THERE TIME

My beloved Mother
there is a distance
between my birth
and my crucifixion
an immense time
some left vague
what was I like
at twelve
was there time
left for me
did you call
out to me
do you remember
those long years
Mother did I smile
back your smile to me
did I run into
your embrace
you held me
in birth and in death
did you hold me
in life
my Mother
I loved you

THIS DAY TO MOURN

Today no birds will fly
nor songs be heard
this day to mourn
Christs Mother died on this day
the skies are the color of lead
and the seas are thick black
during melancholy dawn
a white whale was sighted
spewing fountains of blood red
an albatross was shrieking
as the waves buried him
scorpions remained
in sand and rock
and storms were abolished
Jesus wished that the air be filled
with his Mothers gentleness
and it was
he spoke in softness to her
take hold of my arm
and we will enter together
blessed eternal moments

LEAVING THE EYES OPEN

The memory of pain
returns the pain
through nightmares of pain
which breaks down sleep
and resists rests possibility
leaving the eyes open
continually recording
its internality and its
non transferability
a screaming out heightens
its subjectivity thus its
objectivityness
seeks internal reality
reduces hope and provokes prayer
yet pain compromises prayers purity
the shock is in the prolonged suffering
it is up to Christ to ease the pain
or to stop it altogether
pain onto death
do not give false hope
that is the Devils property
Gods realm is to provide

a true sanctuary from pain
when pain is deliberately caused
by evil and torturers
it is God that must pursue them
to the ends of the Earth
to see destruction of evils pain
is mans right and Gods responsibility
pain is so internally private that
it shocks the normal into anguished tears
the great cathedrals absorb pains travail
when the organs thunderous sound
blanks out memory
by the ever present
exaggeration of the decibels
pains vibrations can not compete
the great hospital orders founded
by the church to ease pain
knowing pains insistence
on its privacy
next to God
the memory of pain
returns the pain

INTERIOR STONES IN THE NIGHT

A golden haired angel
covered in a gown
of blue and white crosses
flew into the cathedral one night
still a black dawn
this angel was sent
to see that the space would be empty
he flew up to the rose window
with a candle in his hand
sweeping the flame across
the diameter of the glass
from the rose window
he flew down the main aisle
searching for life
he found an old man seated
on a wooden chair
when the man saw the angel
he was neither surprised
or discomforted
the angel alighted by his side
the man spoke to the angel
I come quite often here
and sit through the night
looking at the shadows
of this great cathedral of stone

angel you are wonderful
when the columns shadows engulf you
what is your name angel
I am called angel
and sir by what name are you named
I am called Rodin and I am a sculptor
I come at night to inhale
the cathedrals magnificence
I await the morning mists
to fill this great church
sometimes I wait till the rose windows
flood the walls and floors
with the colors from Heaven
angel you are beautiful
what brings you here
this mornings night
I await Jesus
tell him I visit his house often
at night and through my very body
have felt his spirit
the angel slowly moved his wings
and glided to the entry doors
I will remember your name
and speak it to my Lord

RESPLENDENT GLORY

Can you imagine all
the cathedrals organs
playing at once
their sound moving
up to the Heavens
so magnificent in scale
that even the angels
stop their flight and
glide to the musics waves
the sound even lifts the clouds
all prayers move between the notes
the flying buttresses stiffen
and the tremendous rose windows oscillate
their colors splashing the stone floors
and silently pass along the walls as
shadows of pigment
and as all the organs fill Gods space
as many women as each organ begin
to sing in resplendent glory
the feminine voice makes the angels
wings flux in harmony
a slight joy is infused within
their bodies and through
the mystical sign of their wings
they awaken God to the beauty upon Earth
and slowly the music and voices fade into
the silence of a landscape at peace
and God adjusts

YOUR CONTEMPLATIVE SADNESS

I have seen
you in all your possible ages
miracles in stone
created by a sculptor
none are your likeness
but all are you
he turned stone into life
breath came out
of your beautiful mouth
I was by your side
as a child
I am resting
on your supportive thigh
you were seated
in your dignity of calmness
he caught a moment
of your distance
in your stoic oriental beauty
our eyes are almost closed
in another Pietà immense
your contemplative sadness
moves from your silent face
to your outstretched hand
the fingers reflecting
a vanished heart
the sculptors Madonna
captures the tautness of youth
and strength of years

and yet and yet
the roughness of old age
a crucified Christ is
depicted as old
why should this be so
the simultaneity of a
young and old death

AND TO SOLITUDE

Baroque church of Prague
I entered your space unseen
I looked up at the ceiling
the painted angels began to stir
they floated to the organs sound
the angels came onto me
and lifted me up
I felt my heart filling
with a Heavenly blood
as we ascended
the thunderous final notes
blew us through all solidities
I breathed in the fragrance
of the angels as we flew up
to the last judgement
and to solitude

CASKETED BONES

We entered in the opal evening
the snow covered cathedral of
Santiago de Compostela
a light grey mist
filled its interior volume
some chapels were bathed
in a charcoal light some purple
escaped through the iron gates
there was no one in the space
we faced the writhing altar piece
figures and objects in entanglement
flesh colors pinks browns blood-reds
darken eyes pure white pupils and
golden shards exploding into nights
silence aftermaths of last judgements
we descended into the place of casketed
bones
we walked rapidly through the stone
cathedral to the entry doors
wrapping our scarves around neck and mouth
we pushed through the doors

we stood in the blackness of night
on the top of the stairs
overlooking the empty square
we heard the wind blowing with a fierceness
behind us inside the cathedral
as we crossed the square
sounds of unearthlyness
followed us which continued through
a sleepless night until dawn
I picked up a feather from the stone floor
and placed it in a wooden lacquered box
which reflected dawns vanishing moon
from my window I looked out
of my room and observed
a figure in the vast square
it appeared to be looking for
something lost

I closed the shutters
and went back to my sleeping wife

59

LET US RETURN

Braque I do look into
the shadows of cathedrals
at night I am searching
for hidden angels they also
may be in the fog of the chapels
towards dawn one time long ago
I awoke in a pew and observed
one of our cathedral nuns
speaking to one of them
the nun knew that I saw them
whispering to one another
I asked sister what language
do they speak our own was her
reply not French as I left the
cathedral I passed a column
where a sculptured angel was
perched Braque I would swear
it was in the image of the one
I had seen with the nun
these cathedrals have many
mysteries within them
you know I sketched many
beautiful women in my studio

some call them my angels
this is not so the name can
not be applied
at some festivals
we dress them up in elaborate
costumes and add wings it is magical
but these are not real angels
admittedly they are very beautiful
the ones like the one speaking to
the nun in the cathedral are very
serious
Rodin I never told you but I did
see one once in a cathedral of night
its robes were in black fabricated
of different rich materials
the feathers of the wings were
in the deepest black as were its
eyes the face of alabaster color
the hair of the purist white
Rodin I believe all you have related
to me let us return to our studios
and work our creations will
outlast us

SOUND OF THE SEA

Braque was listening
to the distant sound of the sea
it became louder
until it burst through the window
where the albatross had
previously entered
the water submerged the room
Braque swam towards the window
he was shocked by what he saw
angels from 14th century paintings
had entered the flooded room
they were slowly flying
in the gelatinous sea water
the liquid quickly receded
leaving the walls under a glaze
the wall was filled with

entrapped angels within
the pattern of the wallpaper
Braque was confronted with
an impossibility
he began to paint frantically
before everything dried
Rodin went down to the beach
scattered in the sand
were all his figures
from the Gates of Hell
he felt Braque
to be in danger
he sensed the beautiful
angels had drowned
and his friend
was painting them

A CHURCH SPIRE ROSE

Braque walked along the Normandy beach
he stopped to look at a plough buried in the sand
its color was vermillion
the seas skies turned charcoal
the wind had picked up he wrapped the scarf
Rodin had given him closer to his body
he continued along the beach
and thought about the white albatross
and the blood on its beak
he bent down to roll the bronze Poseidon on its back
the black empty eye sockets penetrated through his heart
he sat looking at the fishing boat plowing through the sea
he remembered his father duplicating a
wallpaper pattern on to a canvas
and the smile the pigment brought to his lips
he moved up to the dunes and encountered
one of Rodins female figures from the Gates of Hell
he kissed her metal lips which softened under his pressure
over the dunes horizon a church spire rose

THE SWEET JUICE BLED

Two young lovers in church
were eating a Tuscan pear
the sweet juice bled
from the corner of her mouth
her cheek reflected
the pale green of the fruit
and the eyes of her beloved
she kissed him sweetly
and thought about
the drunken Bacchus
of Michelangelo and the grapes
of faun and the luster of marble
her spring intimate thought
of kisses given in churches

the Mothers kiss for her daughters
first communion
the lifting of the veil
for the marriage kiss
the grandsons kiss for
his departed grandmother
the kissing of the baptismal child
the priest at mass
kissing the crucifix
the kiss of Judas
in a painting on the church wall
the parishioners kissing
their fingers after

the sign of the Cross
the Mother of Christ
kissing her son
after the deposition
the kisses given upon
the statues of Jesus
a kiss given on a prayer book
the kiss given by the stained glass
to the interior of a church
and all other unknown
and secret kisses

OF SHADES AND SHADOWS

He went from
cathedral to cathedral
and waited for the night
it poured in throughout
the space and volumes
as a cacophony of shades and shadows
he sat and contemplated
the monochromatic nuances
the thickness of air
was different in each church
he distinguished the blacks
and the grays
and followed the stone column lines
till they sprung into arches
and disappeared in the darkness above
he adjusted his heavy winter coat
and folded his hands in his lap
he imagined the flying buttresses
in the moonlight and the beech trees
on the hills of France as the rivers slept
he thought of the women he sketched
in his studio made of iron
he told everyone that the rose windows
were charcoal black in mornings night
he preferred a womans breast
to the laugh of a gargoyle
somehow he equated a solid cut stone
with the curvature of a womans supple body

in their nakedness he celebrated their reality
sometimes he fell asleep in the cathedral
and was gently awakened by a nun
he spoke to her of the miraculous light
of Frances mornings and pointed out
the carved lilies in the wood pews
he thought about his Gates of Hell
and the possibility that it was
all taking place in a storm at sea
he walked across a gravel courtyard
to his room overlooking the base
of a buttress and a stone saint
a young woman in a plum colored scarf
was moving through an old snow
his eyes followed her
till she turned a corner
of the ageing cathedral

IT HARDLY FLOWED

The emptiness
of Christs tomb
matched the emptiness
of his Mothers heart
her sorrow drowned
in the blood of her
hearts chamber
it hardly flowed
they searched
everywhere
in the caves chamber
until belief set in
his departure was complete
the inevitability of
resurrection and ascension
the last judgement to be
glory in arrival
his word kept

YOUR ANGUISH BURNING

How am I to reconcile
the landscapes I have
seen you in
from Jerusalem to Assisi
from Judean hill
to Tuscan valley
you seemed so fragile
overlooking the Dead Sea
dry simple just beginning
even sparse barren
after a snow
you are singular alone
without color perhaps sepia
a fading monochrome
the Cross stark
surrounded by gray ochre
building and sky
Galilee without blue
the nails driven by stone

your anguish burning
with the sun
when in Italy you are filled
with color
burnt umber to sienna red
profusion of pigment
the robes cloth painted
black purple gold
silver edged
and your flesh
colors unimaginable
the crucifixion
the deepest blood red
and night rendered black
the sun orange the moon yellow
your soul could not be painted
it pervades all Earth
and Heavens landscapes
in time

IN TIME OVER LONG TIME

In the beginning
it is your Mother
who moves us
with her virgin birth
her blue shawl protects
you . . . you are partially revealed
unaware of the wise men's gifts
somehow the reflecting pieces
are out of place
Jerusalem casts opacities
even the lemon trees cast shadows
someone cuts a lemon in the darkness
the juice at first is bitter
the soul knows its taste
it takes time and gives time
why is it that it is in
Byzantium that the woman
Mother of Christ dominates
the mosaics and the icons
Jesus emerges slowly
the steppes of Russia must be crossed
the white churches with onion domes

await patiently Christs distant journey
the Eastern church priest
swings in slow motion the smoke filled containers
the Mother of the holy child
stares with her circular eyes in amazement
at the trumpeting angels announcing
the placement of mosaic piece by piece
then the thunderous shift through the Po valley
over the mountains and the beginning of all
construction church and cathedral
throughout the blessed land
and the crucifix at once is everywhere
and forgiveness is made possible
the story of Christs journey is passed on
mouth to mouth and the northern passes are opened
in time over long time stone is laid upon stone
and the cathedrals of France are built
and the Virgin is celebrated
and her light moves
through the great rose windows
facing the altars above which is her son

HIS SOUL WAS DANCING

I know that he
sat in the cathedral at night
and looked into the shadows
his eyes focused
on the recesses of space
shadow and shade
caressed the stone surfaces
he thought about those buried
in the stone floor below
the candles gave light
to the tapestries
capturing deep blues and blood reds
in his studio of metal skylights
he drank wine
with his models
he observed their plum soft skin

they smiled when he touched their earrings
once he sketched one in church
leaning her shoulder on a stone column
she was gazing at the rose window
in the daylight he blew her a kiss
her shadow moved across the floor
as a horizontal compass
her body curves as contours
one evening he closed his eyes
and listened for the music of the angels
he imagined how it was made
they flew in agitation
their wings produced intersecting sound waves
he within his soul was dancing
with one of his young women
from his Gates of Hell

68

AND WHAT ARE THEY

Braque and Rodin
first met while each was walking
on the beach below the cliffs
of Le Havre
Rodin immediately began to
describe the young women
he sketched in his studio
and how he loved them
their forms and their shapes
Braque asked Rodin how he felt
when they became bronzes stones
and marbles Rodin replied
the same but in a different way
it is one thing when I run my fingers
over their soft pliable skin
and I breath in their aroma
I keep my eyes on them open
look the sea is becoming very rough
when these young women of France

become marble I run my hands
all over their hard bodies with my eyes closed
the women of bronze present another sensation
I run my lips over the metal and taste their curvatures
Braque the sea wind is becoming stronger and you
your still lifes interest me
Braque speaks look out to the seas horizon
some day I will paint this blue black sky
below the cliffs of Le Havre
Rodin you visit cathedrals at night
yes to see the Virgin and hear the angels sing
I keep notes on their revelations
and what are they
my God the cathedrals themselves
and what do you paint
I paint still lifes
and albatrosses flying through wallpaper
so that one day I may paint the undersea itself

69

THE CLIFFS OF LE HAVRE

O Braque of Normandy!
your contemplative gaze
at the cliffs of Le Havre
painted into the chapel in Ronchamp
where the mists pass behind the Virgin Mary
and the double pulpit welcomes nights morning
and a rose is placed on the stark altar
and a gray vase enters your composition
antiquity and pears are celebrated
O Braque of Normandy!
your Fathers wallpaper inculcated your still soul
your elongated hand Toledos anticipation
Rilke knew of your sea meeting with Rodin
you placed the pear next to your guitar
it was then that Rodin spent the nights
in the great cathedrals searching the shadows
it was then that you exploded the harbor into stones

O Braque of Normandy!
you almost entered a devils pact
when you speared a torn sheet of music with a T-square
your three bathers entered the dark Atlantic
a few years before the poet drew blood from a rose
who were your massive women with small breasts
your secrets will be kept by the painter and his model
your premonition was the still life with skull
O Braque of Normandy!
silent before a crucifix easel
hide your dead black birds
your flowers of evil were placed in a vase
your abandoned bicycle rusts in the sand
your Indochina gray bird stands tall
your anchor thrown at the night drowns
the Greeks knew your sea birds
O Braque of Normandy!

IN THE SPRING

He climbed the hill of sorrows
carrying a crucifix of roses
he planted it in the Earth
each red petal fell to the ground
their accumulation appeared to be
a mound of blood
what remained was the thorns
wrapped around the wood Cross
snow fell and buried the rose petals
in the spring all would be taken away
the echoes of all the laments
would hover six inches above
the saddened Earth and finally
die down to a whisper
and then he would be gone

THE AIR BECAME COLD

In the far distance
there seemed to be
a great turbulence in the sky
the clouds had become black
within them sparks of gold
the agitation became more visible
the points of color more primary
and then and then they came into view
hundreds of flying angels blocking out the sun
throwing an immense shadow over the plateau
the noise of their wings produced discordant
chilling sounds the air became cold
their voices were like nothing on Earth
a pitch of the highest intensity
they were moving towards the resurrection

PURE BLUE WAS SAVED

The blue sky suddenly
became elevational and gold leaf
the slowly moving clouds stopped
and became pigment white
and the angels rushed in
and pushed against and filled the frame
some had to abandon the space
some figures had to change size
so they could possibly fit
a place of pure blue was saved
for the Virgin Mary
its edging was sienna red
God with a stroke of his hand
split the wood icon in half
creating an open space
where Christ could make his
ascension

DEATH OF THE VIRGIN

When her soul
left her
content

THE FUNERAL OF JAN PALACH

When I entered the first meditation,
  I escaped the gravity of the object,
I experienced the emptiness,
  And I have been dead a long time.

When I had a voice you could call a voice,
  My mother wept to me:
My son, my beloved son,
  I never thought this possible,

I'll follow you on foot.
  Halfway in mud and slush the microphones picked up.
It was raining on the houses;
  It was snowing on the police-cars.

The astronauts were weeping,
  Going neither up nor out.
And my own mother was brave enough she looked
  And it was all right I was dead.

—David Shapiro

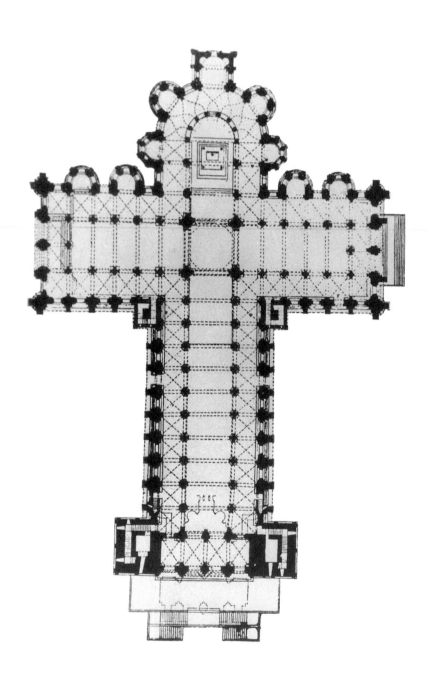

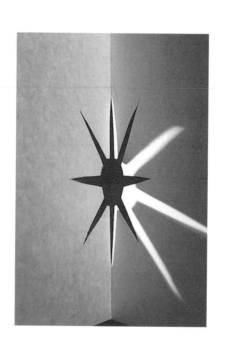

ILLUSTRATIONS

COVER AND PAGE 125

Santiago de Compostela. Cathedral (c.1078)
Interior, Nave toward East, Triforum level
Lantern Slide Collection, The Irwin S. Chanin School of Architecture Archive
of The Cooper Union for the Advancement of Science & Art.

PAGE 1

Santiago de Compostela. Cathedral (c.1078)
Exterior, South Transept Portal, Transfiguration detail
Lantern Slide Collection, The Irwin S. Chanin School of Architecture Archive
of The Cooper Union for the Advancement of Science & Art.

PAGE 124

Santiago de Compostela. Cathedral (c.1078)
Ground plan
Lantern Slide Collection, The Irwin S. Chanin School of Architecture Archive
of The Cooper Union for the Advancement of Science & Art.

PAGE 126

Wedding of the Moon and Sun. Chapel (1998)
Courtesy John Hejduk, architect. Steven Hillyer, photographer.

127